# The ESSE

MW00835570

# MECHANICS II

## Staff of Research and Education Association, Dr. M. Fogiel, Director

> This book is a continuation of *"THE ESSENTIALS OF MECHANICS I"* and begins with Chapter 12. It covers the usual course outline of Mechanics II. Earlier/basic topics are covered in *"THE ESSENTIALS OF MECHANICS I"*. More advanced topics will be found in *"THE ESSENTIALS OF MECHANICS III"*.

Research and Education Association
505 Eighth Avenue
New York, N.Y. 10018

# THE ESSENTIALS OF MECHANICS II

Printed in the United States of America

Library of Congress Catalog Card Number 87-61798

International Standard Book Number 0-87891-612-1

# WHAT "THE ESSENTIALS" WILL DO FOR YOU

This book is a review and study guide. It is comprehensive and it is concise.

It helps in preparing for exams, in doing homework, and remains a handy reference source at all times.

It condenses the vast amount of detail characteristic of the subject matter and summarizes the **essentials** of the field.

It will thus save hours of study and preparation time.

The book provides quick access to the important facts, principles, theorems, concepts, and equations of the field.

Materials needed for exams, can be reviewed in summary form — eliminating the need to read and re-read many pages of textbook and class notes. The summaries will even tend to bring detail to mind that had been previously read or noted.

This "ESSENTIALS" book has been carefully prepared by educators and professionals and was subsequently reviewed by another group of editors to assure accuracy and maximum usefulness.

Dr. Max Fogiel
Program Director

# CONTENTS

This book is a continuation of *"THE ESSENTIALS OF MECHANICS I"* and begins with Chapter 12. It covers the usual course outline of Mechanics II. Earlier/basic topics are covered in *"THE ESSENTIALS OF MECHANICS I"*. More advanced topics will be found in *"THE ESSENTIALS OF MECHANICS III"*.

# CHAPTER 12

# KINEMATICS OF PARTICLES

## 12.1 BASIC DEFINITIONS

Rectilinear Motion - The resulting linear motion of a particle when influenced by the resultant force whose direction and line of action always remain the same.

Position:

Fig. 12·1

The equation of motion is given as a scalar function of time t, $x = x(t)$.

Instantaneous velocity: $v = \dfrac{dx}{dt}$ (12.1)

Instantaneous acceleration:

$$a = \frac{dv}{dt} = \frac{d}{dt}\left(\frac{dx}{dt}\right) = \frac{d^2x}{dt^2}$$ (12.2)

Curvilinear Motion - Resulting non-linear motion of a particle when influenced by a variable force.

Position:

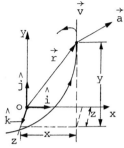

Fig. 12·2

The position is described by vector $\vec{r}$, $\vec{r} = \vec{r}(t)$.

Velocity:

$$\vec{v} = \frac{d\vec{r}}{dt} = \dot{\vec{r}}$$

(12.3)

Acceleration:

$$\vec{a} = \frac{d\vec{v}}{dt} = \dot{\vec{v}}$$

(12.4)

In terms of rectangular components:

Position:

$$\vec{r} = x\hat{i} + y\hat{j} + z\hat{k}$$

(12.5)

Velocity:

$$\vec{v} = \frac{d\vec{r}}{dt} = \dot{x}\hat{i} + \dot{y}\hat{j} + \dot{z}\hat{k}$$

(12.6)

Acceleration:

86

$$\vec{a} = \frac{d\vec{v}}{dt} = \ddot{x}\hat{i} + \ddot{y}\hat{j} + \ddot{z}\hat{k} \qquad (12.7)$$

Centroidal Motion - Center of gravity remains stationary. Only a moment couple is acting on the body.

Speed - The magnitude of the velocity vector:

$$v = |\vec{v}| = \sqrt{\dot{x}^2 + \dot{y}^2 + \dot{z}^2} \qquad (12.8)$$

Hodograph - A curve generated by the tip of the velocity vector. A chord of the hodograph is the change in velocity during the corresponding time.

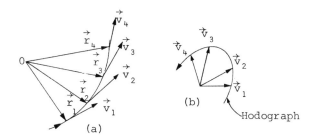

Fig. 12·3 Hodograph

# 12.2 MOTION OF A PARTICLE

The motion of a particle is known if its position is known for all values of time t.

Case 1: If acceleration is given in terms of t, a = f(t):

Velocity:   dv = adt

$$v - v_0 = \int_0^t f(t)dt \qquad (12.9)$$

87

Gives v in terms of t

Position:

$$x = \int_0^t v(t)dt + x_0 \qquad (12.10)$$

Case 2: If acceleration is a function of velocity, $a = f(v)$:

Time: $\quad f(v) = \dfrac{dv}{dt}$

$$t = \int \frac{dv}{f(v)} + t_0 \qquad (12.11)$$

Position: $\quad f(v) = v \dfrac{dv}{dx}$

$$x = \int \frac{vdv}{f(v)} + x_0 \qquad (12.12)$$

Case 3: If acceleration is a function of displacement, $a = f(x)$:

Velocity:

$$vdv = adx$$
$$\frac{1}{2} v^2 - \frac{1}{2} v_0^2 = \int_{x_0}^x f(x)dx \qquad (12.13)$$

Position:

$$x = \int_0^t v \, dt + x_0 \qquad (12.14)$$

# 12.3  UNIFORM MOTION

A) For constant velocity:

$$\boxed{x = x_0 + vt}$$
(12.15)

B) For constant acceleration:

$$\begin{array}{l} v = v_0 + at \\[6pt] x = x_0 + v_0 t + \dfrac{1}{2} at^2 \\[6pt] v^2 = v_0^2 + 2a(x-x_0) \end{array}$$
(12.16)

$x_0, v_0$  are initial values for x and v.

# 12.4  RELATIVE MOTION

**Rectilinear Motion**

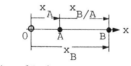

Fig. 12·4

$$\begin{array}{l} \text{Relative position:} \quad x_B = x_A + x_{B/A} \\[6pt] \text{Relative velocity:} \quad v_B = v_A + v_{B/A} \\[6pt] \text{Relative Acceleration:} \quad a_B = a_A + a_{B/A} \end{array}$$
(12.17)

Note:

A) All motion is measured from the same origin.

B) Time is recorded at the same instant.

**Dependent Motion**

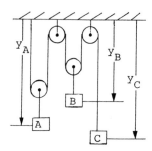

Fig. 12·5

Relative position:   $2x_A + 2x_B + x_C = $ Constant

Relative velocity:   $2v_A + 2v_B + v_C = 0$

Relative acceleration:   $2a_A + 2a_B + a_C = 0$

(12.18)

**Curvilinear Motion**

Relative position:   $\vec{r}_B = \vec{r}_A + \vec{r}_{B/A}$

Relative velocity:   $\vec{v}_B = \vec{v}_A + \vec{v}_{B/A}$   (12.19)

Relative acceleration:   $\vec{a}_B = \vec{a}_A + \vec{a}_{B/A}$

**Absolute Motion**  – Motion with respect to a fixed frame of reference.

# 12.5  GRAPHICAL SOLUTIONS

Graphical solutions are useful when:

A) Data is obtained from experiments.

B) When the position, velocity, and acceleration are not analytical functions of time t.

C) The motion is made up of different parts.

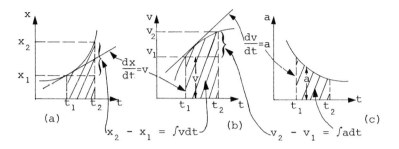

Fig. 12·6 Graphical Solutions

Relationship between the graphs:

A) Slope of the x-t curve represents velocity.

B) Slope of the v-t curve represents acceleration.

C) Area under the a-t curve represents the change in velocity.

D) Area under the v-t curve represents the change in position.

**Special Cases:**

A) Constant Velocity:

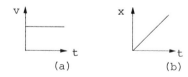

Fig. 12·7 Constant Velocity

B) Constant Acceleration:

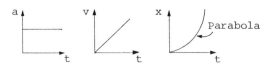

Fig. 12·8 Constant Acceleration

## C) Linear Acceleration:

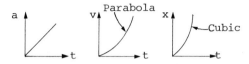

Fig. 12·9 Linear Acceleration

In general, if the acceleration is a polynomial of degree n, then the velocity will be a polynomial of degree n+1, and the position will be a polynomial of degree n+2. These polynomials will be represented by graphs of curves of the same degree.

### Moment—Area Method

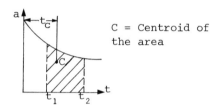

C = Centroid of the area

Fig. 12·10

If the value of $t_c$ is known, then

$$x_2 = x_1 + v_1 t_1 + (\text{area under the a-t curve})(t_2 - t_c)$$

(12.20)

Using the v-x curve to find acceleration:

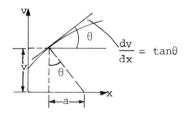

$$\frac{dv}{dx} = \tan\theta$$

Fig. 12·11

$$a = v \frac{dv}{dx} = v \tan \theta \qquad (12.21)$$

# 12.6 TANGENTIAL AND NORMAL COMPONENTS

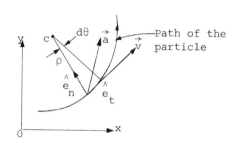

Fig. 12·12

c = Center of curvature of the path

$\hat{e}_t$ = Unit vector in the direction of the velocity vector

$\hat{e}_n$ = Unit vector in the direction normal to the velocity

$$\frac{d\hat{e}_t}{dt} = \dot{\theta}\hat{e}_n = \frac{v}{\rho}\hat{e}_n, \text{ where}$$

$$\rho = \frac{(1+(dy/dx)^2)^{3/2}}{\left|\frac{d^2y}{dx^2}\right|}$$

$\rho$ = radius of curvature of the path

$(12.22)$

Velocity:

$$\vec{v} = v\hat{e}_t \qquad (12.23)$$

Acceleration:

$$\vec{a} = \dot{v}\hat{e}_t + \frac{v^2}{\rho}\hat{e}_n \qquad (12.24)$$

There are two parts to equation (12.24):

Tangential Acceleration:

$$a_t = \dot{v} \qquad (12.25)$$

Centripetal Acceleration:

$$a_n = \frac{v^2}{\rho} \qquad (12.26)$$

Magnitude of Total Acceleration: $|\vec{a}| = \sqrt{\dot{v}^2 + \frac{v^4}{\rho^2}}$ $\qquad(12.27)$

Special cases:

A) If the particle is traveling at constant speed:

$$\vec{a} = \frac{v^2}{\rho}\hat{e}_n; \quad a_t = 0$$

B) If the particle is in rectilinear motion:

$$\vec{a} = \dot{v}\,\hat{e}_t; \quad a_n = 0$$

Correlation between rectangular components with normal and tangential components of $\vec{a}$:

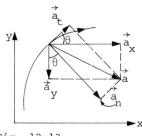

Fig. 12·13

94

$$a_n = a_x \sin\theta + a_y \cos\theta$$
$$a_t = a_x \cos\theta - a_y \sin\theta$$

(12.28)

or

$$a_x = a_n \sin\theta + a_t \cos\theta$$
$$a_y = a_n \cos\theta - a_t \sin\theta$$

(12.29)

# 12.7 RADIAL AND TRANSVERSE COMPONENTS

**Polar Coordinates**

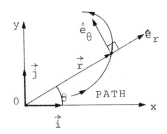

Fig. 12·14

$\hat{e}_r$ = Radial Unit Vector

$\hat{e}_\theta$ = Transverse Unit Vector

Unit Vector Derivatives:

$$\frac{d\hat{e}_\theta}{dt} = -\dot{\theta}\,\hat{e}_r$$

$$\frac{d\hat{e}_r}{dt} = \dot{\theta}\,\hat{e}_\theta$$

(12.30)

$$\text{Position: } \vec{r} = r\hat{e}_r$$

$$\text{Velocity: } \vec{v} = \dot{r}\hat{e}_r + r\dot{\theta}\hat{e}_\theta$$

$$\text{Acceleration: } \vec{a} = (\ddot{r} - r\dot{\theta}^2)\hat{e}_r + (r\ddot{\theta} + 2\dot{r}\dot{\theta})\hat{e}_\theta$$

(12.31)

| Radial Components: | Transverse Components: |
|---|---|
| Velocity: $v_r = \dot{r}$ | Velocity: $v_\theta = r\dot{\theta}$ |
| Acceleration: $a_r = \ddot{r} - r\dot{\theta}^2$ | Acceleration: $a_\theta = r\ddot{\theta} + 2\dot{r}\dot{\theta}$ |
| | $\qquad = \dfrac{1}{r}\dfrac{d}{dt}(r^2\dot{\theta})$ |

Transformation into Tangential and Normal Components:

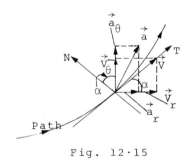

Fig. 12·15

$$a_t = a_r\cos\alpha + a_\theta\sin\alpha = \frac{a_r v_r + a_\theta v_\theta}{v}$$

$$a_n = a_\theta\cos\alpha - a_r\sin\alpha = \frac{a_\theta v_r - a_r v_\theta}{v}$$

(12.32)

## Cylindrical Coordinates

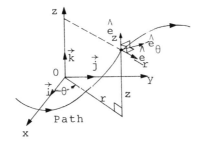

Fig. 12·16

Unit vector derivatives as given by equation (12.30):

$$\frac{d\hat{e}_r}{dt} = \dot{\theta}\,\hat{e}_\theta$$

$$\frac{d\hat{e}_\theta}{dt} = -\dot{\theta}\,\hat{e}_r$$

Position: $\vec{r} = r\hat{e}_r + z\hat{e}_z$

Velocity: $\vec{v} = \dot{r}\hat{e}_r + r\dot{\theta}\hat{e}_\theta + \dot{z}\hat{e}_z$

Acceleration: $\vec{a} = (\ddot{r} - r\dot{\theta}^2)\hat{e}_r + (2\dot{r}\dot{\theta} + r\ddot{\theta})\hat{e}_\theta + \ddot{z}\,\hat{e}_z$

(12.33)

Transformation:

$$\hat{e}_r = \vec{i}\cos\theta + \vec{j}\sin\theta$$

$$\hat{e}_\theta = -\vec{i}\sin\theta + \vec{j}\cos\theta$$

$$\hat{e}_z = \vec{k}$$

(12.34)

## Spherical Coordinates

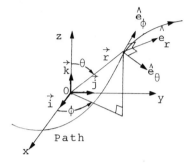

Fig. 12·17

Unit Vector Derivatives:

$$\frac{d\hat{e}_r}{dt} = \dot{\phi}\hat{e}_\phi \sin\theta + \dot{\theta}\hat{e}_\theta$$

$$\frac{d\hat{e}_\theta}{dt} = -\dot{\theta}\hat{e}_r + \dot{\phi}\hat{e}_\phi \cos\theta \qquad (12.35)$$

$$\frac{d\hat{e}_\phi}{dt} = -\dot{\phi}\hat{e}_r\sin\theta - \dot{\phi}\hat{e}_\theta\cos\theta$$

Position: $\vec{r} = r\hat{e}_r$

Velocity: $\vec{v} = \hat{e}_r\dot{r} + \hat{e}_\phi r\dot{\phi}\sin\theta + \hat{e}_\theta r\dot{\theta}$

Acceleration: $\vec{a} = (\ddot{r} - r\dot{\phi}^2\sin^2\theta - r\dot{\theta}^2)\hat{e}_r$

$$+ (r\ddot{\theta} + 2\dot{r}\dot{\theta} - r\dot{\phi}^2\sin\theta\cos\theta)\hat{e}_\theta$$

$$+ (r\ddot{\phi}\sin\theta + 2\dot{r}\dot{\phi}\sin\theta + 2r\dot{\theta}\dot{\phi}\cos\theta)\hat{e}_\phi$$

(12.36)

Transformation:

$$\hat{e}_r = \vec{i} \sin\theta \cos\phi + \vec{j} \sin\theta \sin\phi + \vec{k} \cos\theta$$
$$\hat{e}_\theta = \vec{i} \cos\theta \cos\phi + \vec{j} \cos\theta \sin\phi - \vec{k} \sin\theta \qquad (12.37)$$
$$\hat{e}_\phi = -\vec{i} \sin\phi + \vec{j} \cos\phi$$

# 12.8 ANGULAR VELOCITY

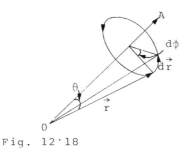

Fig. 12·18

For a particle rotating about an axis $\overline{OA}$ through an angle $d_\phi$:

$$d\vec{r} = d\phi(\hat{e} \times \vec{r}) \qquad (12.38)$$

The angular velocity is defined by:

$$\vec{\omega} = \dot{\phi}\,\hat{e} \qquad (12.39)$$

The velocity of the particle is then expressed as:

$$\vec{v} = \dot{\vec{r}} = \vec{\omega} \times \vec{r} \qquad (12.40)$$

Angular velocity vectors obey the rule of vector addition.

99

# CHAPTER 13

# KINETICS OF PARTICLES

## 13.1 LINEAR MOMENTUM

Linear momentum is defined as

$$\boxed{\vec{P} = m\vec{v}}$$  (13.1)

It is directed in the same direction as the vector $\vec{v}$.

Results:

A) Newton's first law can be written as:

If the resultant force acting on a particle is zero, then the linear momentum $\vec{P}$ of the particle is constant. This is the Law of Conservation of Linear Momentum.

B) Newton's second law can be expressed as

$$\Sigma \vec{F} = \frac{d}{dt}(m\vec{v}) = \frac{d\vec{P}}{dt}$$

i.e., the resultant force is equal to the rate of change of linear momentum.

C) Newton's third law:

For two particles A and B,

$$\vec{P}_A + \vec{P}_B = \text{constant}$$

# 13.2 EQUATIONS OF MOTION

**Rectangular Components**

$$\Sigma\,(F_x\vec{i} + F_y\vec{j} + F_z\vec{k}) = m(a_x\vec{i} + a_y\vec{j} + a_z\vec{k})$$

or

$$
\begin{aligned}
\Sigma F_x &= m\ddot{x}\\
\Sigma F_y &= m\ddot{y}\\
\Sigma F_z &= m\ddot{z}
\end{aligned}
\tag{13.2}
$$

**Tangential and Normal Components**  (refer to Figure 12.12)

$$
\begin{aligned}
\Sigma\,F_t &= ma_t = m\,\frac{dv}{dt}\\[2mm]
\Sigma\,F_n &= ma_n = m\,\frac{v^2}{\rho}
\end{aligned}
\tag{13.3}
$$

$\rho$ = Radius of curvature of the path

**Radial and Transverse Components**  (refer to Figure 12.14)

$$
\begin{aligned}
\Sigma F_r &= ma_r = m(\ddot{r} - r\dot{\theta}^2)\\
\Sigma F_\theta &= ma_\theta = m(r\ddot{\theta} + 2\dot{r}\dot{\theta})
\end{aligned}
\tag{13.4}
$$

# 13.3 DYNAMIC EQUILIBRIUM

A particle is in dynamic equilibrium if the sum of all forces acting on the particle, including inertial forces, is equal to zero:

$$\Sigma\,\vec{F} - m\vec{a} = 0 \tag{13.5}$$

The term $-m\vec{a}$ is called the inertia vector.

The first term $\Sigma\vec{F}$ is sometimes called effective forces. i.e., it is the resultant of all external forces.

When expressed in tangential and normal form:

A) The tangential compoment of inertia measures the resistance of the particle to change in speed.

B) The normal component of inertia, also called centrifugal force, measures the resistance of the particle to leave its curved path.

# 13.4 VELOCITY-DEPENDENT FORCE

The force acting on a particle can be a function of time. Some examples of such forces are:

A) Viscous resistance

B) Air resistance

General equation:

$$\vec{F}(v) = m\, \frac{d\vec{v}}{dt} \qquad (13.6)$$

Equation 13.6 can be integrated to solve for time:

$$t_2 - t_1 = \int_1^2 \frac{m}{\vec{F}(\vec{v})}\, d(\vec{v}) \qquad (13.7)$$

A second integration yields position:

$$x_2 - x_1 = \int_1^2 v(t)\, dt \qquad (13.8)$$

Terminal Velocity - When the drag force is equal to the weight of the body there is no acceleration and no increase in velocity.

A) Linear Case - Assume the fluid resistance is proportional to the first power of velocity. The differential equation of motion:

$$-(mg+cv) = m\frac{dv}{dt} \qquad (13.9)$$

where g = gravitational constant and c is a function of viscosity and geometry of the object. If c is constant then,

$$v = -\frac{mg}{c} + \left(\frac{mg}{c} + v_0\right)e^{-ct/m} \qquad (13.10)$$

where $v_0$ = initial velocity.

As the t → ∞, equation 13.10 becomes

$$\boxed{v_t = -\frac{mg}{c}} \qquad (13.11)$$

$v_t$ is the terminal velocity.

A second integration of equation 13.9 yields:

$$x-x_0 = \int_0^t v(t)dt = -\frac{mg}{c}t + \left(\frac{m^2g}{c^2} + \frac{mv_0}{c}\right)(1-e^{-ct/m}) \qquad (13.12)$$

Characteristic time is defined as:

$$\tau = \frac{m}{c} \qquad (13.13)$$

By using equation 13.13 and 13.11, equation 13.10 becomes:

$$v = -v_t + (v_t+v_0)e^{-t/\tau} \qquad (13.14)$$

B) Quadratic Case - If the fluid resistance is proportional to the square of velocity.

Differential equation of motion:

$$\boxed{-mg \pm cv^2 - m\frac{dv}{dt}} \qquad (13.15)$$

Note: A double sign ($\pm$) is necessary for any even power of v.

Solving equation 13.15 for time:

Upward Motion: $t = \int \dfrac{mdv}{-mg-cv^2} = -\tau \tan^{-1}\dfrac{v}{v_t} + t_0$

Downward Motion:

$t = \int \dfrac{mdv}{-mg+cv^2} = -\tau \tanh^{-1}\dfrac{v}{v_t} + t_0{}^*$

(13.16)

where
$t_0, t_0{}^*$ = Initial time and are not necessarily equal

$$v_t = \sqrt{\dfrac{mg}{c}} = \text{Terminal Velocity}$$ (13.17)

and

$$\tau = \sqrt{\dfrac{m}{cg}} = \text{Characteristic Time}$$ (13.18)

Solve for velocity v:

Upward Motion: $v = v_t \tan \dfrac{t_0-t}{\tau}$

Downward Motion:

$v = -v_t \tanh \dfrac{t-t_0{}^*}{\tau}$

(13.19)

If $t_0 = 0$, then $t_0{}^* = 0$ and

$$v = -v_t \tanh \dfrac{t}{\tau} = -v_t \left( \dfrac{e^{t/\tau}-e^{-t/\tau}}{e^{t/\tau}+e^{-t/\tau}} \right)$$ (13.20)

According to the definition of the hyperbolic tangent, i.e.,

$$\sinh z = \frac{e^z - e^{-z}}{2} \; ;$$

$$\cosh z = \frac{e^z + e^{-z}}{2} \implies \tanh z = \frac{e^z - e^{-z}}{e^z + e^{-z}}$$

# 13.5 ANGULAR MOMENTUM

Angular momentum is defined as the moment about the origin O of the angular momentum vector $m\vec{v}$. It is denoted by $\vec{H}_0$:

$$\boxed{\vec{H}_0 = \vec{r} \times m\vec{v}} \qquad (13.21)$$

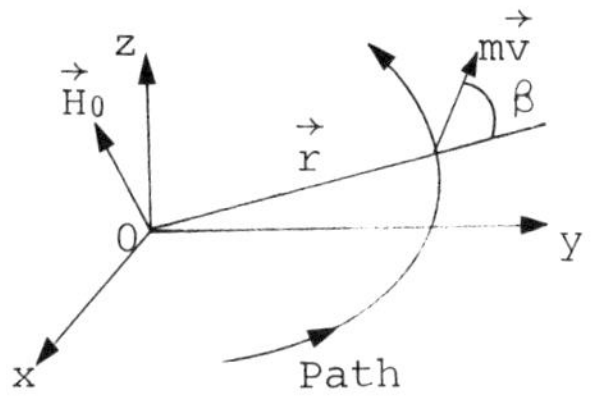

Fig. 13·1

Note: The angular momentum vector acts in a direction perpendicular to the plane containing the position and the linear momentum vectors.

The scalar form of equation 13.21 is

$$\boxed{H_0 = rmv \sin \beta} \qquad (13.22)$$

Determinant form:

$$\vec{H}_0 = \begin{vmatrix} \vec{i} & \vec{j} & \vec{k} \\ x & y & z \\ mv_x & mv_y & mv_z \end{vmatrix} \qquad (13.23)$$

105

Compoment form by expanding equation 13.23:

$$H_x = m(yv_z - zv_y)$$
$$H_y = m(zv_x - xv_z)$$
$$H_z = m(xv_y - yv_x)$$

(13.24)

In terms of polar coordinates:

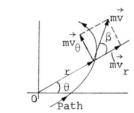

Fig. 13·2

$$H_0 = mr^2\dot{\theta}$$

(13.25)

By Newton's second law:

$$\Sigma\vec{M}_0 = \dot{\vec{H}}_0,$$

(13.26)

i.e., the vector sum of the moments about O, acting on the particle equals the time derivative of the moment of momentum, or angular momentum, of the particle about O.

# 13.6  CENTRAL FORCE FIELDS

Central Force - The force acting on a particle which is directed towards or away from a fixed point O called the center of force. The particle is considered to be moving in a central force field. The magnitude of the force depends on the distance between the particle and the point O.

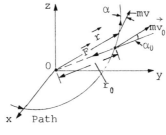

Fig. 13·3

The angular momentum of a particle moving in a central force field is constant:

$$\vec{r} \times m\vec{v} = \vec{H}_0 = \text{constant} \qquad (13.27)$$

Conservation of angular momentum:

$$rmv \sin\alpha = r_0 mv_0 \sin\alpha_0 \qquad (13.28)$$

$r_0, v_0$, and $\alpha_0$ are initial parameters.

In terms of polar coordinates (Figure 13.2), equation (13.25), the angular momentum per unit mass is:

$$h = r^2\dot\theta \qquad (13.29)$$

Areal Velocity:

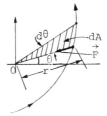

Fig. 13·4

Areal velocity is defined as:

$$dA/dt$$

Areal Velocity

$$\frac{dA}{dt} = \frac{1}{2} r^2 \frac{d\theta}{dt}$$

For a particle under a central force field, the areal velocity is constant.

Newton's Law of Gravitation

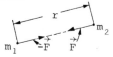

Fig. 13.5

G = universal constant

$$\boxed{F = G \frac{m_1 m_2}{r}}$$

(13.30)

Trajectory of Central Force Motion

Governing equations in radial and transverse compoments:

$$m(\ddot{r} - r\dot{\theta}^2) = -F$$

$$M(r\ddot{\theta} + 2\dot{r}\dot{\theta}) = 0$$

(13.31)

Using equation (13.29), and introducing a new function $u = \frac{1}{r}$, the differential equation of motion for central force fields is:

$$\boxed{\frac{d^2u}{d\theta^2} + u = \frac{F}{mh^2u^2}}$$

(13.32)

# 13.7  SPACE MECHANICS

For satellite motion, equation (13.32) takes the form:

$$\boxed{\frac{d^2u}{d\theta^2} + u = \frac{GM}{h^2}}$$ (13.33)

where
M = Mass of the Earth

m = Mass of the Satellite

r = Distance from the Earth's Center
   to the satellite

$u = \frac{1}{r}$

G = Gravitational Constant

Solution of equation 13.33:

$$\boxed{\frac{1}{r} = u = \frac{GM}{h^2} + c \cos \theta}$$ (13.34)

c = Constant of Integration

This is an equation of a conic section in polar coordinates.

Eccentricity, e: Ratio of the distance between satellite and earth to the distance between the satellite from a fixed line.

$$\boxed{e = \frac{c}{GM/h^2} = \frac{ch^2}{GM}}$$ (13.35)

Therefore, equation 13.34 can be rewritten as

$$\boxed{\frac{1}{r} = \frac{GM}{h^2}(1 + e \cos \theta)}$$ (13.36)

Three cases for orbits

A) e > 1:

Two solutions result, $\theta_1$ and $-\theta_1$, the orbit is a hyperbola.

B) e = 1.

The radius becomes infinite for $\theta = 180°$, the orbit is a parabola.

C) $e < 1$:

The orbit is an ellipse.

For the special case when $e = 0$, the orbit is a circle.

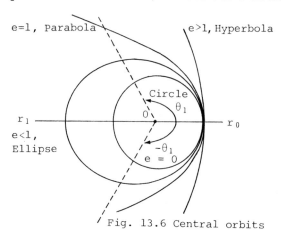

e=1, Parabola

e>1, Hyperbola

Circle

$r_1$
e<1,
Ellipse

$\theta_1$

$O$

$-\theta_1$
$e = 0$

$r_0$

Fig. 13.6 Central orbits

Assume that the satellite begins its free flight at the vertex ($r_0$) of its orbit, with velocity parallel to the surface of the earth:

Angular Momentum:

$$h = r_0^2 \, \dot{\theta}_0 = r_0 v_0$$

(13.37)

Constant c:

$$c = \frac{1}{r_0} - \frac{GM}{h^2}$$

(13.38)

Orbits by Velocity:

For a parabolic trajectory, let $c = GM/h^2$ in equation (13.38), and eliminate h between equations (13.37) and (13.38):

$$v_p = \sqrt{\frac{2GM}{r_0}}$$

(13.39)

For a hyperbolic trajectory:

$$v > v_p$$

For an elliptic trajectory:

$$v < v_p$$

110

For a circular trajectory ($c=0$):

$$v_{cir} = \sqrt{\frac{GM}{r_0}} = \sqrt{\frac{gR^2}{r_0}}$$ (13.40)

where

g = Acceleration due to gravity at earth's surface

R = Earth's Radius

Escape Velocity - The smallest velocity required for a satellite to escape the earth's gravitational field and not return to its starting point.

The escape velocity, $v_{esc}$, is the same as the velocity for a parabolic trajectory:

$$v_{esc} = \sqrt{\frac{2GM}{r_0}} = \sqrt{\frac{2gR^2}{r_0}}$$ (13.41)

Perigee - A point on the satellite's orbit closest to earth.

Apogee - A point on the satellite's orbit farthest from the earth.

Perihelion - A point on the planet's orbit closest to the sun.

Aphelion - A point on the planet's orbit farthest from the sun.

**Orbital Parameters**

Let $v_0$ be the velocity at $\theta = 0$.

$$\text{Eccentricity } e = (v_0/v_{cir})^2 - 1$$ (13.42)

Equation of the orbit:

$$r = r_0 \frac{(v_0/v_{cir})^2}{1+[(v_0/v_{cir})^2-1]\cos\theta}$$ (13.43)

$$\text{Apogee or Aphelion Distance } r_1 = r_0 \frac{(v_0/v_{cir})^2}{2-(v_0/v_{cir})^2}$$

$$(13.44)$$

Period – The time required for a satellite to complete an orbit. Denoted by $\tau$

$$\tau = ca^{3/2}$$

$$(13.45)$$

where $c = 2\pi(GM)^{-\frac{1}{2}}$

      $a$ = Semimajor Axis

In terms of Geometry:

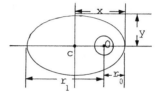

Fig. 13·7

$$\tau = \frac{2\pi xy}{h}$$

$$(13.46)$$

# 13.8 KEPLER'S LAWS

Kepler's Laws of Planetary Motion

First Law:

    Every planet moves in its orbit such that the line joining it to the sun sweeps over equal areas in equal intervals of time regardless of the line's length.

Second Law:

    The orbit of every planet is an ellipse with the sun at one of its foci.

Third Law:

The square of the period of any planet is directly proportional to the cube of the semi-major axis of its orbit.

Notes:

A) The first and third laws result from the inverse-square law.

B) The second is a consequence of the fact that planetary motion is central, and is usually written in the form $dA/dt$ = constant.

Angular Momentum and Kepler's Second Law:

$$\frac{dA}{dt} = \frac{H_0}{2m} = \text{constant} \qquad (13.47)$$

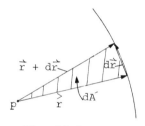

Fig. 13·8

# 13.9 INVERSE-SQUARE REPULSIVE FIELDS

Inverse-Square Repulsive Field - A central force field in which the direction of the force on a particle is away from the origin. The magnitude of this force is proportional to the inverse square of the distance between the origin and the particle.

The deflection of atomic particles by the nuclei is used as an example of the inverse-square repulsive field:

Coulomb's Law:  $F(r) = \frac{Qq}{r^2}$

113

where  Q = Charge of the Larger Particle

q = Charge of the Smaller Particle

r = Distance Between the Particles.

Let Q be the origin of the system.

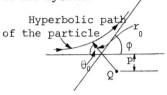

Fig. 13·9

Differential Equation of the Path:

$$\frac{d^2u}{d\theta^2} + u = -\frac{Qq}{mh^2} \ , \qquad u = \frac{1}{r}$$

(13.48)

Solution of Equation (13.48) is:

$$r = \frac{1}{u} = \frac{1}{A\cos(\theta - \theta_0) - Qq/mh^2}$$

(13.49)

This is a hyperbolic orbit.

An alternate form of the solution, i.e., equation (13.49):

$$r = \frac{mh^2 Q^{-1}q^{-1}}{-1 + (1 + 2Emh^2 Q^{-2}q^{-2})^{\frac{1}{2}}\cos(\theta - \theta_0)}$$

(13.50)

where:

$$E = \text{Energy} = \frac{1}{2}mv^2 + \frac{Qq}{r}$$

From angle relationships, we have the scattering formula:

$$\tan\theta_0 = \sqrt{2Em}\ Q^{-1}q^{-1}h = \cot\frac{\phi}{2}$$

(13.51)

114

To express h in terms of the impact parameter P (see Figure 13.9):

$$h = |\vec{r} \times \vec{v}| = Pv_0$$

where
$v_0$ = Initial Speed of the Particle.

From the fact that:

A) Energy is constant

B) Kinetic energy $E = \frac{1}{2} mv_0^2$

C) Inital potential energy = 0 ($r = \infty$)

The scattering formula, equation (13.51), can be rewritten as:

$$\boxed{\cot \frac{\phi}{2} = \frac{Pmv_0^2}{Qq} = \frac{2PE}{Qq}}$$ (13.52)

# 13.10 NEARLY CIRCULAR ORBITS

Stability - The tendency of a particle in a central force in its initial circular orbit after sustaining a slight disturbance in its motion.

Radial Equation of Motion:

$$m\ddot{r} - \frac{mh^2}{r^3} = F(r)$$

If the orbit is circular, the equation becomes

$$-mh^2/c^3 = F(c),$$

where c is the radius of the circle.

Let y = r-c, and expand the y+c terms in powers of y:

$$\boxed{m\ddot{y} + [-\frac{3}{c} F(c) - F'(c)]y = 0}$$ (13.53)

115

where higher order terms are taken at zero.

Conditions for Stability:

A) If the coefficient of y is greater than 0, then the motion is stable.

B) If the coefficient of y is less than 0, then the motion is not stable.

C) If the coefficient y equals zero, then higher order terms of the expansion must be considered to determine stability.

Therefore, the circular orbit of radius c is stable if:

$$F(c) + \frac{c}{3} F'(c) < 0 \qquad (13.54)$$

Special case: If $F(r) = -kr^a$, then the orbit is stable if $a > -3$.

Apsides and Apsidal Angles

Apsis or Apse - The extremal radius in an orbit.

Note: In planetary orbit, the apsides are known as the aphelion (maximum) and perihelion (minimum).

Apsidal Angle - The angle formed by two consecutive apsides (Figure 13.10).

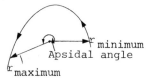

Fig. 13·10

Nearly circular motion (given a stable orbit about r=c):

A) The period is

$$\tau = 2\pi \sqrt{\frac{m}{-[\frac{3}{2} f(c) + f'(c)]}} \qquad (13.55)$$

116

B) The apsidal angle is

$$\beta = \frac{1}{2}\tau\dot{\phi} = \pi\left[3 + \frac{cF'(c)}{F(c)}\right]^{-\frac{1}{2}}$$

(13.56)

C) If $F(r) = -kr^a$,

$$\beta = \pi(a+3)^{-\frac{1}{2}}$$

(13.57)

Observations:

A) $\beta$ is not a function of the orbit size.

B) For $a = -z(\beta=\pi)$ and $a=1(\beta=\pi/2)$, the orbit is said to be repetitive.

C) If there is a slight deviation from the inverse-square law, then, according to the deviation from $\pi$ in the apsidal angle, the apsides will either move forward or regress.

Special case: If $F(r) = -\left(\dfrac{A}{r^2} + \dfrac{B}{r^4}\right)$, and B is very small, then:

$$\beta = \pi\left(1 + \frac{B}{Ac^2}\right),$$

(13.58)

where higher order terms are neglected.

Results:  1) If $B < 0$, the apsides regress

2) If $B > 0$, the apsides move forward

# CHAPTER 14

# ENERGY AND MOMENTUM METHODS-PARTICLES

## 14.1 WORK OF A FORCE

Given a particle on a space curve c at a point R, in an inertial reference frame, and at point S at some instant later, with position vectors $\vec{r}_1$ and $\vec{r}_2$, respectively. Then the work done by a force F through a displacement dr of the particle is defined as

$$dw = \vec{F} \cdot d\vec{r} \qquad (14.1)$$

Note: Work in S.I. units is expressed in N·m (Joule); in Figure 14.1 U.S. cutomary units, work is expressed in ft-lb or lb-in.

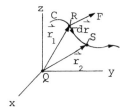

Fig. 14·1

Work for a finite distance from point 1 to point 2 is defined as the line integral:

$$w_{1-2} = \int_1^2 \vec{F} \cdot d\vec{r} \qquad (14.2)$$

118

Work of a constant force (in linear motion):

$$w_{1-2} = F \cos\theta \cdot \Delta y$$

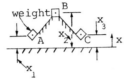

Fig. 14·2

Work done by a weight:

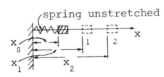

Fig. 14·3

$$
\begin{aligned}
w_{A-B} &= -\text{weight}(x_2 - x_1), \\
w_{B-C} &= -\text{weight}(x_3 - x_2), \\
w_{A-C} &= -\text{weight}(x_3 - x_1)
\end{aligned}
\qquad (14.3)
$$

If $x_3 = x_1$, then $w_{A-C} = 0$.

Work of Springs

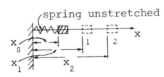

Fig. 14·4

$$w_{1 \to 2} = \frac{1}{2} k x_1^2 - \frac{1}{2} k x_2^2 \qquad (14.4)$$

k = Spring constant or stiffness of the spring force exerted by the spring on the mass: $F = kx$

119

Work of a Gravitational Force - Given two particles of masses $M_1$ and $M_2$ such that $M_1$ is stationary and is at a distance $\rho_1$ from $M_2$ at A; while $M_2$ moves along c to point B, and at a distance $\rho_2$ from $M_1$. Then, the work of the gravitational force $\vec{F}$ from A to B is

$$w_{A-B} = -\int_{\rho_1}^{\rho_2} \frac{GM_1M_2}{\rho^2} d\rho = GM_1M_2 \left[ \frac{1}{\rho_1} - \frac{1}{\rho_2} \right] \qquad (14.5)$$

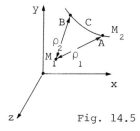

Fig. 14.5

# 14.2 WORK-ENERGY PRINCIPLE

Kinetic energy for a particle of mass M and velocity v is defined as

$$K.E. = \frac{1}{2} mv^2 \qquad (14.6)$$

Kinetic energy is the energy possessed by a particle by virtue of its motion.

Principle of Work and Energy - Given that a particle undergoes a displacement under the influence of a force $\vec{F}$, the work done by $\vec{F}$ equals the change in kinetic energy of the particle.

$$w_{1-2} = (KE)_2 - (KE)_1 \qquad (14.7)$$

120

Note: Since this principle is a consequence of Newton's second law, it is valid only in an inertial reference system.

Results of the Principle of Work and Energy

A) Acceleration is not necessary and may not be obtained directly by this principle.

B) The principle may be applied to a system of particles if each particle is considered separately.

C) Those forces that do not contribute work are eliminated.

Kinetic Energy and Newton's Law:

$$F = mv \frac{dv}{dx} = \frac{d}{dx}(KE),$$

where KE is a function of x.

# 14.3 POWER AND EFFICIENCY

Power is defined as the time-rate of change of work and is denoted by dw/dt,

$$\boxed{Power = \frac{dw}{dt} = \vec{F} \cdot \vec{v}} \qquad (14.8)$$

In the SI system of units, power has units J/S or watt (W) (W not to be confused with the lower case w, denoting work). In the U.S. customary system, power is in ft-lb/s or horsepower (H.p.).

Note: 1 h.p. = 550 ft-lb/s and 1 h.p. = 746 W.

Mechanical Efficiency:

$$\boxed{\eta = \frac{Power\ out}{Power\ in}} \qquad (14.9)$$

where both numertor and denominator must have the same

units. It is assumed that the rate of work is constant.

Note: Since power out < power in, $\eta$ is always less than 1.

# 14.4 CONSERVATIVE FORCES

as
The del operator - denoted by the symbol $\vec{\nabla}$ is defined

$$\vec{\nabla} = i \frac{\partial \phi}{\partial x} + j \frac{\partial \phi}{\partial y} + k \frac{\partial \phi}{\partial z} \qquad (14.10)$$

in rectangular coordinates.

The gradient of a scalar function is defined as:

$$\vec{\nabla} \phi = \text{grad}\phi = \frac{\partial}{\partial x} i + \frac{\partial}{\partial y} j + \frac{\partial}{\partial z} k \qquad (14.11)$$

If a force $\vec{F}$ is expressible as the gradient of a scalar function $\phi$,

$$\text{i.e.,} \qquad \vec{F} = -\vec{\nabla}\phi \qquad (14.12)$$

then F is known as a conservative force and $\phi$ is the potential function.

Note: The gradient represents a forcing action.

Conservative Force - Work done by a particle under the action of this force is independent of the path followed by the particle.

Results:
A) If $\vec{F}$ is conservative, then $\vec{F} = \vec{\nabla}\phi$
B) If $\vec{F} = -\vec{\nabla}\phi$, then

$$\int_1^2 \vec{F} \cdot d\vec{r} = \int_1^2 -\left(\frac{\partial \phi}{\partial x} dx + \frac{\partial \phi}{\partial y} dy + \frac{\partial \phi}{\partial z} dz\right)$$

$$= \int_1^2 -d\phi = \phi(x_1, y_1, z_1) - \phi(x_2, y_2, z_2)$$

(14.13)

where $\phi$ is a scalar function in cartesian coordinates. Hence, the work of $\vec{F}$ is an exact differential, and independent of the path.

C) If $\vec{F} = -\vec{\nabla}\phi$, then

$$\oint_c \vec{F} \cdot d\vec{r} = 0$$

(14.14)

i.e., the work of a conservative force for any closed path is zero.

D) If $F = -\vec{\nabla}\phi$, then curl $\vec{F} = 0$, or $\vec{\nabla} \times \vec{F} = 0$; the reverse is also true, i.e., if $\vec{\nabla} \times \vec{F} = 0$, then $\vec{F}$ is conservative.

Existance of a Potential Function - The necessary and sufficient conditions for $\phi$ to exist may be expressed in cartesian coordiantes as

$$\frac{\partial F_x}{\partial y} = \frac{\partial F_y}{\partial x}, \quad \frac{\partial F_z}{\partial x} = \frac{\partial F_x}{\partial z},$$

$$\frac{\partial F_z}{\partial y} = \frac{\partial F_y}{\partial z}$$

(14.15)

# 14.5 POTENTIAL ENERGY

Potential Energy - In general, it is the stored energy of a

body or particle in a force field associated with its postiion from a reference frame.

Potential Energy and Work - If potential energy is denoted by PE, then

$$U_{1-2} = (PE)_1 - (PE)_2 \qquad (14.16)$$

where PE = weight (x), see Figure 14.3. A negative value of $U_{1-2}$ is associated with an increase in potential energy.

Potential Energy for Space Vehicles:

$$
\begin{aligned}
(PE)_g &= -G\,\frac{M_1 M_2}{r} \\
&= -\frac{\text{weight}}{r}\,R^2 ,
\end{aligned}
\qquad (14.17)
$$

where     $M_1$ = Mass of the Earth

$M_2$ = Mass of the object (space vehicle, satellite, etc.)

R = The Radius of the earth, "weight" as measured on the surface of the earth

r = The distance between centers of $M_1$ and $M_2$.

The potential energy and work for a spring are given by:

$$U_{1-2} = PE_1 - PE_2 \qquad (14.18)$$

where PE = $\frac{1}{2} ky^2$, and is known as the potential energy with respect to the elastic force.

Notes:

A) If $U_{1-2} < 0$, then the potential energy increases.

B) The work $U_{1-2}$ of the elastic force is a function of the final and initial deflections of the spring.

Potential energy methods may be utilized when the forces involved are conservative.

# 14.6 GRAVITATIONAL POTENTIAL

Gravitational potential is defined as

For a system $\quad \phi = G \dfrac{M_1 M_2}{r}$

$$\phi = \frac{(PE)_g}{M_1} = -G \frac{M_2}{r} \qquad (14.19)$$

For a particle of Mass $M_2$

Gravitational Field Intensity – Ratio of the gravitational force on a particle to the mass of that particle:

$$\vec{G} = \frac{\vec{F}(r)}{m} \qquad (14.20)$$

Relationship between $\vec{G}$ and $\phi$:

$$\vec{G} = -\vec{\nabla} \phi \qquad (14.21)$$

Specific Cases:

## A) Uniform Spherical Shell

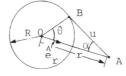

Fig. 14·6

$$\phi_A = -G \frac{2\pi \rho^2 R}{rR} \int_{r-R}^{r+R} du = \frac{-GM}{r} \qquad (14.22)$$

$\rho$ = Density of the Sphere

Note:

1) The gravitational field outside the shell is the same as if the entire mass was concentrated at the center O.

2) The potential inside the shell is constant and the field is zero.

## B) Thin Ring

Using Figure 14.4 again:

$$\Phi_A = -G \int \frac{dM}{u} = -G \int_0^{2\pi} \frac{\mu R \, d\theta}{u} \tag{14.23}$$

where   $\mu$ = Linear Density of the Ring

By use of geometry:

$$\Phi_A = -G \frac{4 \, \mu R}{r} \, k \left( \frac{R}{r} \right) \tag{14.24}$$

k = Complete Elliptic Integral

$$k \left( \frac{R}{r} \right) = \int_0^{\pi/2} \left[ 1 - \left( \frac{R}{r} \right)^2 \sin^2 \alpha \right]^{-\frac{1}{2}} d\alpha \tag{14.25}$$

Equation 14.24 can also be expressed in terms of a series:

$$\Phi_A = \frac{-GM}{r} \left( 1 + \frac{R^2}{4r^2} + \ldots \right) \tag{14.26}$$

Field Intensity:

$$\vec{G} = -\frac{\partial \Phi}{\partial r} \hat{e}_r = \left( \frac{-GM}{r^2} - \frac{3GMR^2}{4r^4} - \ldots \right) \hat{e}_r \tag{14.27}$$

This field is not inverse-square. But for large distances, the field is predominantly inverse-square. This is true for a finite body of any shape.

Potential in a General Central Field

A general isotropic central field is expressed as:

$$\vec{F} - F(r)\hat{e}_r \qquad (14.28)$$

If the field is conservative, $\vec{\nabla} \times \vec{F} = 0$, and:

$$PE = \int_r^\infty F(r)\,dr \qquad (14.29)$$

The force function is given by:

$$F(r) = -\frac{\partial v(r)}{\partial r} \qquad (14.30)$$

# 14.7 CONSERVATION OF ENERGY

## A) Conservative Case

For a particle under the action of conservative forces:

$$(KE)_1 + (PE)_1 = (KE)_2 + (PE)_2 = E \qquad (14.31)$$

The sum of kinetic and potential energy at a given point is constant.

Equation (14.31) can be written as:

$$E = \frac{1}{2} mv^2 + (PE) \qquad (14.32)$$

127

Equation (14.32) can be solved to give the motion of the particle as:

$$v = \pm \sqrt{\frac{2}{m} [E - (PE)]}$$  (14.33)

or in an integral form:

$$\int \frac{\pm\, dx}{\sqrt{\frac{2}{m} [E - v(x)]}} = t$$  (14.34)

Turning Points:

The potential function (PE) must be less than or equal to the total energy E:

$$(PE) \le E$$

From equation (14.32), speed v must become zero when (PE) = E. The particle must stop and reverse its direction of motion at this point. These points are called turning points.

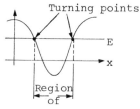

Fig. 14·7

## B) Nonconservative Case

When nonconservative forces are present in a system:

$$\text{Total Force} = \vec{F} + \vec{F}'$$

where $\vec{F}$ = Conservative Forces

$\vec{F}'$ = Nonconservative Forces

Relating potential and kinetic energy with the nonconservative force F',

$$d(PE + KE) = \int \vec{F}' \cdot d\vec{r} \qquad (14.35)$$

Note:

    1) The direction of $\vec{F}'$ is opposite to that of $d\vec{r}$.

    2) Total energy E decreases with motion.

    3) Friction forces are nonconservative.

# 14.8 APPLICATION TO SPACE MECHANICS

Consider the motion of a satellite:

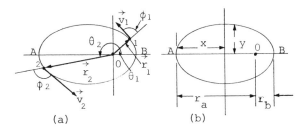

(a)            (b)

Fig. 14·8

Work done from point 1 to point 2:

$$w_{1 \to 2} = GMm \left( \frac{1}{r_2} - \frac{1}{r_1} \right) \qquad (14.36)$$

Change in kinetic energy from 1 to 2:

$$(KE)_{1 \to 2} = \frac{1}{2} m(v_2^2 - v_1^2) \qquad (14.37)$$

Conservation of Energy:

$$\frac{1}{2} mv_1^2 - \frac{GMm}{r_1} = \frac{1}{2} mv_2^2 - \frac{GMm}{r_2} \qquad (14.38)$$

Conservation of Angular Momentum:

$$r_1 m v_1 \sin \phi_1 = r_2 m v_2 \sin \phi_2 \qquad (14.39)$$

Note: The extremal values of v and r occur when $\phi = 90°$.

Special Case:

If the satellite is moving in a circular orbit with constant velocity:

Gravitational Pull = Centrifugal Inertia Force

or

$$v^2 = \frac{GM}{r} \qquad (14.40)$$

Geometry:

Refer to Figure 14.8(b):

$$x = \frac{1}{2}(r_a + r_b)$$

$$y = \sqrt{r_a r_b} \qquad (14.41)$$

Areal Velocity:

$$\frac{dA}{dt} = \frac{1}{2} r v \sin \phi \qquad (14.42)$$

Polar Coordinates

**A) Central Force Field**

Energy Equation:

$$\frac{1}{2} m h^2 \left[ \left( \frac{du}{d\theta} \right)^2 + u^2 \right] + PE = E \qquad (14.43)$$

where $\quad u = \frac{1}{r},$

$h = rv$ and PE is a function of $\frac{1}{u}$.

## B) Inverse-Square Field

Potential Function:

$$PE = -\frac{k}{r} = -ku \qquad (14.44)$$

$$K = constant$$

Energy Equation:

$$\frac{1}{2}mh^2\left[\left(\frac{du}{d\theta}\right)^2 + u^2\right] - ku = E \qquad (14.45)$$

Solution of equation (14.45):

$$u = \frac{k}{mh^2}\left[1 + \sqrt{(1+2Emh^2k^{-2})}\cos\theta\right] \qquad (14.46)$$

or, in terms of r:

$$r = \frac{mh^2k^{-1}}{1 + \sqrt{(1+2Emh^2k^{-2})}\cos\theta} \qquad (14.47)$$

Eccentricity in terms of total energy may be expressed as:

$$e = (1 + 2Emh^2k^{-2})^{\frac{1}{2}} \qquad (14.48)$$

Classification of Orbits:

$$E < 0 \quad or \quad (e < 1): \qquad Ellipse$$
$$E = 0 \quad or \quad (e = 1): \qquad Parabolic$$
$$E > 0 \quad or \quad (e > 1): \qquad Hyperbolic$$

In general:

$$KE < |PE| \quad for \ closed \ orbits$$
$$KE \geq |PE| \quad for \ open \ orbits$$

# 14.9 IMPULSE AND MOMENTUM

Impulse-Momentum Method - An alternate method to solve problems in which forces are expressed as functions of time. It is applicable to situations when forces act over a small interval of time.

Linear Impulse-Momentum Equation:

$$\int_1^2 \vec{F}\, dt = \text{impulse} = m\vec{v}_2 - m\vec{v}_1 \qquad (14.49)$$

Figure (14.9) expresses the idea that the vector sum of the initial momentum and impulse equals the final momentum of the particle.

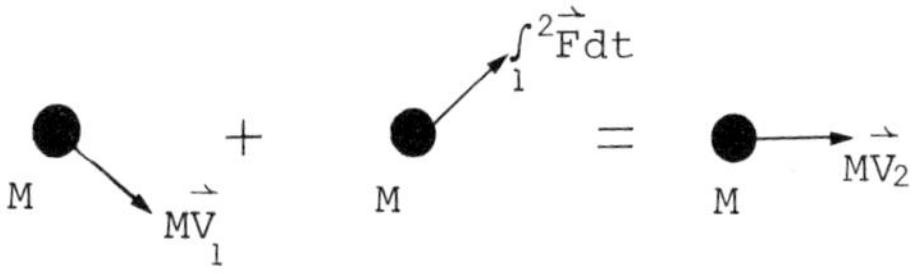

Fig. 14·9

Impulse is a vector quantity and acts in the direction of the force if the force remains constant.

$$\int_1^2 \vec{F}\, dt = \vec{i} \int_1^2 F_x\, dt + \vec{j} \int_1^2 F_y\, dt + \vec{k} \int_1^2 F_z\, dt \qquad (14.50)$$

To obtain solutions, it is necessary to replace equation (14.49) with its compoment equations.

When several forces are involved, the impulse of each force must be considered:

$$m\vec{v}_1 + \Sigma \int_1^2 \vec{F}\, dt = m\vec{v}_2 \qquad (14.51)$$

When a problem involves more than one particle, each particle must be considered separately and then added:

$$\Sigma m\vec{v}_1 + \Sigma \int_1^2 \vec{F}\, dt = \Sigma m\vec{v}_2 \qquad (14.52)$$

If there are no external forces, conservation of total momentum results:

$$\boxed{\Sigma m\vec{v}_1 = \Sigma m\vec{v}_2} \qquad (14.53)$$

Note: There are cases in which an impulse is exerted by a force which does no work on the particle. Such force should be considered when applying the principle of impulse and momentum in solving problems.

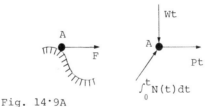

Fig. 14·9A

E.g. Figure (14.9A)

W - Weight of Particle A

F - Horizontal Force

t - Time Taken

N - Normal Force

Here the normal force N does no work but creates an impulse $\int_0^t N(t)\,dt$ on the particle A.

# 14.10 IMPULSE MOTION

Impulsive Force - A very large force acting on a particle over a very short time interval and produces a significant change in momentum.

Impulse-Momentum equation, equation (14.51), becomes:

$$M \vec{v_1} + \Sigma \vec{F} \Delta t = M\vec{v_2}$$

(14.54)

Note: $\Sigma \vec{F} \Delta t$ may also be denoted as $\hat{P}$.

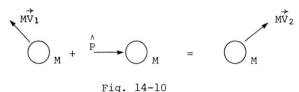

Fig. 14-10

Any force which is non-impulsive may be neglected in equation (14.54), e.g., weight, or small forces.

Unknown forces should be included, e.g., reactive forces (recoil, etc.).

Ideal impulse produces an instantaneous change in momentum and velocity of the particle without producing any displacement.

# 14.11 IMPACT

Impact - Collision of two bodies.

Types of Impact

A) Central Impact - When the line of impact passes through the center of mass of the colliding bodies.

B) Eccentric Impact - When the line of impact does not pass through the center of mass of the colliding bodies.

Two Types of Central Impacts:

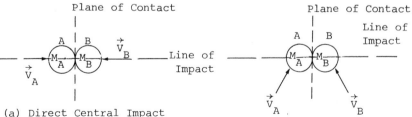

Fig. 14-11 Types of Central Impacts

Total Linear Momentum is Conserved Under Impact:

$$M_A \vec{v}_A + M_B \vec{v}_B = M_A \vec{v}'_A + M_B \vec{v}'_B \qquad (14.55)$$

where $\vec{v}_A, \vec{v}_B$ are velocities before impact and

$\vec{v}'_A, \vec{v}'_B$ are velocities after impact.

Energy Balance:

$$\frac{1}{2} M_A v_A^2 + \frac{1}{2} M_B v_B^2 = \frac{1}{2} M_A {v'_A}^2 + \frac{1}{2} M_B {v'_B}^2 + q$$

$$(14.56)$$

where q = Net Energy Change (deformations, heat, etc.)

Endoergic Impact - When q > 0, representing an energy loss.

Exoergic Impact - When q < 0, representing an energy gain.

Perfectly Elastic Impact - When q = 0, or when e = 1.

## A) Direct Central Impact

Coefficient of restitution:

$$e = \frac{v'_B - v'_A}{v_B - v_A} \qquad (14.57)$$

Equations (14.55) and (14.57) are used simultaneously to solve for $v'_A$ and $v'_B$.

Sign Convention:

Right-Positive; Left-Negative.

Special Cases:

a) e = 0, perfectly plastic impact:

Both particles stay together after impact and move

with the same velocity v'.

Momentum Equation:

$$M_A v_A + M_B v_B = (M_A + M_B) v'$$ (14.58)

b) e = 1, perfectly elastic impact

$$v'_B - v'_A = v_A - v_B$$ (14.59)

Relative velocities are equal before and after impact. Total energy and momentum is conserved.

In most impact cases, e < 1. Total energy is not conserved. The energy loss, q, is expressed as:

$$q = \frac{1}{2} \lambda v_R^2 (1-e^2),$$ (14.60)

where

$$\lambda = \frac{1}{M_A} + \frac{1}{M_B}$$ and is known as the reduced mass,

and

$$v_R = |v_B - v_A|,$$ is the relative speed before impact.

Final Velocities:

$$v_A' = \frac{(M_A + M_B e) v_A + (M_B - e M_B) v_B}{M_A + M_B}$$

(14.61)

$$v_B' = \frac{(M_A - M_A e) v_A + (M_B + e M_A) v_B}{M_A + M_B}$$

## B) Oblique Central Impact

Because $v_A'$ and $v_B'$ are unknowns in both directions and magnitude, four independent equations are needed:

a) The sum of the momentum of particles A and B is

136

conserved in the x direction.

b) The momentum of each particle A and B is conserved in the y direction.

c) The relative velocity of the particles after impact in the x direction equals the product of their relative velocity before impact in the x-direction by the coefficient of restitution.

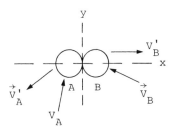

Oblique Central
Impact
Fig. 14-12

## Center of Mass Coordinates:

Two Systems:

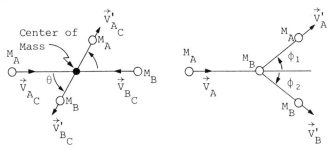

(a) Center of Mass System

(b) Laboratory System

Fig. 14-13

Energy Equation:

$$\frac{\vec{P'}_A^2}{2\lambda} = \frac{\vec{P'}_A^2}{2\lambda} + q$$

(14.62)

$\lambda$ = Reduced Mass

Velocity Relationships:    Refer to Figure 14.14

$$\vec{v}_{A_c} = \vec{v}_A - \vec{v}_{cm} = \frac{M_B \vec{v}_A}{M_A + M_B}$$

(14.63)

$\vec{v}_{cm}$ = Velocity of the Center of Mass

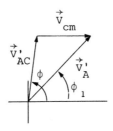

Fig. 14-14

Scattering Angles:

$$\tan \psi_1 = \frac{\sin \phi}{\mu + \cos \phi}$$

$$\mu = \frac{v_{cm}}{v_{A_c}'} = \frac{M_A v_A}{v_{A_c}'(M_A + M_B)}$$

(14.64)

For Elastic Impact:

$$\mu = \frac{M_A}{M_B}$$

(14.65)

Special Cases:

A) If $M_B \gg M_A$, then $\mu$ is small

$\tan \psi_1 \approx \tan \phi$, scattering angles in the laboratory and in the center of mass system are almost equal

B) $M_A = M_B$ then $\mu = 1$

$$\tan \psi_1 = \tan \frac{\phi}{2} \; ; \quad \text{or} \quad \psi_1 = \frac{\phi}{2}$$

The particles will leave the point of contact at right angles when seen in the laboratory system.

For the general case of non-elastic impact:

$$\mu = \frac{M_A}{M_B} \left[ 1 - \frac{q}{KE} \left( 1 + \frac{M_A}{M_B} \right) \right]^{-\frac{1}{2}} \qquad (14.66)$$

KE = Kinetic energy of the incident particle in the laboratory system.

Relation Between Impulse and Coefficient of Restitution:

$$e = \frac{\hat{P}_r}{\hat{P}_c} \qquad (14.67)$$

where
$$\hat{P}_r = M_A \vec{v}_A{'} - M_A \vec{v}_0$$

$$\hat{P}_c = M_A \vec{v}_0 - M_a \vec{v}_a$$

$v_0$ is the velocity during the time when the two particles are in contact with each other.

# 14.12 METHODS OF SOLUTION

Thus far, three distinct methods have been presented to solve kinetics problems:

1) Newton's Second Law of Motion: $\Sigma \vec{F} = m\vec{a}$

2) Method of Work and Energy

3) Method of Impulse and Momentum

Except for short impact phases, most problems involve conservative forces. These problems, in general, have three parts:

1) Impact Phase Parts - Use the method of impulse and momentum. (Secton 14.9 - 14.11)

2) Parts that involve the determination of normal forces -

Use Newton's Laws. (Section 12.1 - 12.8)

3) All Other Parts - Use the method of work and energy. (Section 13.1 - 14.8)

# 14.13 MOTION OF A PROJECTILE

The projectile motion is a classical problem of particle dynamics.

Two Cases:

A) No Air Resistance

Differential Equation of Motion:

$$M \frac{d^2\vec{r}}{dt^2} = - Mg\vec{k}$$

(14.68)

with initial velocity, $v_i = 0$.

Energy Equation:

$$\frac{1}{2} Mv_i^2 = Mgz + \frac{1}{2} M \left[ \left(\frac{dx}{dt}\right)^2 + \left(\frac{dy}{dt}\right)^2 + \left(\frac{dz}{dt}\right)^2 \right]$$

$$v^2 = v_i^2 - 2gz$$

(14.69)

Velocity:

$$\vec{v} = \frac{d\vec{r}}{dt} = -gt\vec{k} + \vec{v}_i$$

(14.70)

Position:

$$\vec{r} = - \frac{1}{2} gt^2 \vec{k} + \vec{v}_i t$$

(14.71)

Trajectory in the x-y plane:

$$y = \frac{\dot{y}_i}{\dot{x}_i} x \qquad (14.72)$$

Equation (14.72) represents a straight line. Value of z in terms of x:

$$
\begin{aligned}
& z = Ax - Bx^2 \\
\text{where} \quad & A = \dot{z}_i / \dot{x}_i \qquad (14.73)\\
& B = g / 2\dot{x}_i^2
\end{aligned}
$$

Equation (14.73) represents a parabola. The trajectory is shown in Figure 14.15:

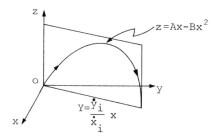

Fig. 14-15 Projectile Motion Without Air Resistance

B) Linear Air Resistance

The motion is now nonconservative.

Force of Resistance $= -Mc\vec{v}$

Differential Equation of Motion:

$$M \frac{d^2\vec{r}}{dt^2} = -Mc\vec{v} - Mg\vec{k} \qquad (14.74)$$

141

Component Form of Equation (14.74)

$$\begin{aligned} \ddot{x} &= -c\dot{x} \\ \ddot{y} &= -c\dot{y} \\ \dot{z} &= -c\dot{z} - g \end{aligned}$$

(14.75)

Velocity Components:

$$\begin{aligned} \dot{x} &= \dot{x}_i e^{-ct} \\ \dot{y} &= \dot{y}_i e^{-ct} \\ \dot{z} &= \dot{z}_i e^{-ct} - \frac{g}{c}(1 - e^{-ct}) \end{aligned}$$

(14.76)

Position Coordinates:

$$\begin{aligned} x &= \frac{\dot{x}_i}{c}(1 - e^{-ct}) \\ y &= \frac{\dot{y}_i}{c}(1 - e^{-ct}) \\ z &= \left(\frac{\dot{z}_i}{c} + \frac{g}{c^2}\right)(1 - e^{-ct}) - \frac{g}{c}t \end{aligned}$$

(14.77)

Vector form of the solution, equation (14.77):

$$\vec{r} = \left(\frac{\vec{V}_0}{c} + \frac{g}{c^2}\vec{k}\right)(1 - e^{-ct}) - \frac{gt}{c}\vec{k}$$

(14.78)

The motion in the x-z plane approaches an asymptote:

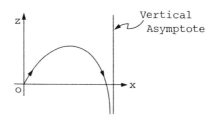

Fig. 14-16 Projectile Motion With
Air Resistance

Approximate Solution - When the air resistance is small.

$$\vec{r} = \vec{v}_0 t - \frac{1}{2} g t^2 \vec{k} - \Delta\vec{r}$$

(14.79)

where

$$\Delta\vec{r} = c \left[ \vec{v}_0 \left( \frac{t^2}{2!} - \frac{ct^3}{3!} + \ldots \right) - g \left( \frac{t^3}{3!} - \frac{ct^4}{4!} + \ldots \right) \vec{k} \right]$$

$\Delta\vec{r}$ can be considered as a correction factor to the zero-resistance case, i.e., Equation (14.71).

# 14.14  MOTION OF A CHARGED PARTICLE

The force exerted on the particle is

$$\vec{F} = q\vec{E}_e$$

(14.80)

where q = Charge of the Particle
$\vec{E}_e$ = Electric Field Strength

Differential Equation of Motion:

$$m \frac{d^2\vec{r}}{dt^2} = q\vec{E}_e$$

(14.81)

m = Mass of the Charged Particle

Component Form of Equation (14.81)

$$m\ddot{x} = qE_{ex}$$
$$m\ddot{y} = qE_{ey}$$
$$m\ddot{z} = qE_{ez}$$

(14.82)

Two Cases:

A) $\vec{E}$ is Uniform and Constant

If the field is directed along the x-axis:

$$\ddot{x} = \frac{qE_e}{m} = \text{constant}$$
$$\ddot{y} = \ddot{z} = 0$$

(14.83)

The path is a parabola. The solutions take the same form as those of the projectile in a uniform gravity field, i.e., Equations (14.70) to (14.73).

If $\vec{E}$ is due to static charges:

$$\vec{\nabla} \times \vec{E}_e = 0$$

(14.84)

The field is conservative and the potential function $\Phi$ exists,

$$-\vec{\nabla}\Phi = \vec{E}_e$$

(14.85)

Energy Equation:

$$E = \frac{1}{2}mv^2 + q\Phi$$

(14.86)

B) Static Magnetic Field $(\vec{B})$ or $\vec{B}$ = Magnetic Induction Vector

144

Force:

$$\boxed{\vec{F} = q\vec{v} \times \vec{B}}$$

(14.87)

Differential Equation of Motion:

$$\boxed{M\frac{d^2\vec{r}}{dt^2} = q(\vec{v} \times \vec{B})}$$

(14.88)

Results:

a) Acceleration is always perpendicular to the direction of motion.

b) Tangential compoment of acceleration $(\dot{v})$ is zero (constant speed).

# 14.15 CONSTRAINED MOTION OF A PARTICLE

Constrained Motion - Motion that is restricted by geometrical constraints. The constraints are assumed to be smooth.

Differential Equation of Motion:

$$\boxed{m\frac{d\vec{v}}{dt} = \vec{F} + \vec{F}_c}$$

(14.89)

where   $\vec{F}$ = External Forces

$\vec{F}_c$ = Force of Constraints

If $\vec{F}$ is conservative, then the energy equation, the equation $E = PE + KE$ can be applied.

Motion of a Curve

Let all parameters be expressed in a single coordinate

s, where s = Distance Measured on the Curve from a Fixed Point.

Energy Equation:

$$\frac{1}{2} m\dot{s}^2 + PE = E$$

(14.90)

Differential Equation of Motion:

$$m\ddot{s} - F_s = 0$$

(14.91)

$F_s$ = Compoment of $\vec{F}$ in the s direction.

Potential Function:

$$F_s = \frac{-d(PE)}{ds}$$

(14.92)

# CHAPTER 15

# SYSTEMS OF PARTICLES

## 15.1 SYSTEMS OF FORCES

For a system consisting of many particles:

Newton's Second Law of Motion takes the form:

$$\sum_{j=1}^{n} \vec{F}_j = \sum_{j=1}^{n} M_j \vec{a}_j \qquad (15.1)$$

Moment equation about an origin O:

$$\sum_{j=1}^{n} (\vec{r}_j \times \vec{F}_j) = \sum_{j=1}^{n} (\vec{r}_j \times M_j \vec{a}_j) \qquad (15.2)$$

The system of external forces, $\vec{F}_j$, and the system of effective forces, $m_j \vec{a}_j$, have the same force and moment result, and are therefore equipollent.

## 15.2 LINEAR AND ANGULAR MOMENTUM

Center of Mass Coordinates:

$$x_{cm} = \frac{\Sigma M_j x_j}{M} \; ; \quad y_{cm} = \frac{\Sigma M_j y_j}{M} \; ; \quad z_{cm} = \frac{\Sigma M_j z_j}{M}$$

(15.3)

Linear Momentum

$$\vec{P} = \sum_{j=1}^{n} M_j \vec{v}_j = M\vec{v}_{cm}$$

(15.4)

Angular Momentum (About the origin O)

$$\vec{H}_0 = \sum_{j=1}^{n} (\vec{r}_j \times M_j \vec{v}_j)$$

(15.5)

Conservation of Momentum

If a system is under no external force of moment, then

$$\Sigma \vec{F} = \dot{\vec{P}} = \sum_{j=1}^{n} (M_j \vec{a}_j) = 0$$

(15.6)

and

$$\Sigma \vec{M}_0 = \dot{\vec{H}}_0 = \sum_{j=1}^{n} (\vec{r}_j \times M_j \vec{a}_j) = 0$$

(15.7)

This means that linear momentum and angular momentum are constant and is the princple of conservation of momentum.

# 15.3 MOTION OF THE MASS CENTER

D'Alembert's Principle:

The vector sum of all external forces acting on a system

of particles is equal to the vector sum of the effective forces acting on all the particles.

$$\sum_{j=1}^{n} \vec{F}_j = \sum_{j=1}^{n} m_j \ddot{\vec{r}}_j = m\vec{a}_{cm} = \dot{\vec{P}}$$  (15.8)

Equation (15.8) defines the motion of the mass center or center of mass.

Properties of the Mass Center:

A) The motion of the mass center is the same as if the total mass of the system and the external forces were concentrated at that point.

B) The center of gravity coincides with the mass center when the weight is taken into consideration.

# 15.4 ANGULAR MOMENTUM ABOUT THE MASS CENTER

When considering the motion of a system of particles, it is sometimes convenient to use a cartesian centroidal frame of reference x'y'z' which translates with respect to the inertial frame or reference xyz.

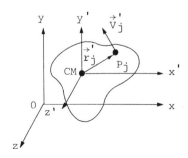

Fig. 15.1

All centroidal coordinates and quantities are denoted by the prime (') notation.

149

Angular momentum in the x'y'z' system:

$$\vec{H}'_{cm} = \sum_{j=1}^{n} (\vec{r}'_j \times m_j \vec{v}'_j) \qquad (15.9)$$

Moment resultant in the x'y'z' system:

$$\sum \vec{M}_{cm} = \dot{\vec{H}}'_{cm} = \sum_{j=1}^{n} (\vec{r}'_j \times m_j \vec{a}'_j) \qquad (15.10)$$

In the xyz system:

$$\vec{H}_{cm} = \sum_{j=1}^{n} (\vec{r}'_j \times m_j \vec{v}_j) \qquad (15.11)$$

Equation (15.9) and (15.11) are equal:

$$\vec{H}_{cm} = \vec{H}'_{cm} \qquad (15.12)$$

Result:

$$\sum \vec{M}_{cm} = \dot{\vec{H}}_{cm}$$

where

$$\vec{H}_{cm} = \sum_{j=1}^{n} (\vec{r}_j \times m_j \vec{v}_j) = \sum_{j=1}^{n} (\vec{r}'_j \times m_j \vec{v}'_j)$$

$$(15.13)$$

Angular momentum may be computed by adding the moments about the center of mass in either the centroidal or inertial reference system.

# 15.5 CONSERVATION OF MOMENTUM

For the mass center CM, the conservation of momentum, equations (15.6) and (15.7) takes the same form:

$$\dot{\vec{P}}_G = 0 \quad \text{or} \quad \vec{P}_G = \text{constant} \qquad (15.14)$$

and

$$\dot{\vec{H}}_G = 0 \quad \text{or} \quad \vec{H}_G = \text{constant} \qquad (15.15)$$

under the conditions of zero resultant external force and moment acting on the system.

Equations (15.14) and (15.15) apply to the system as a whole and never to its compoment parts.


# 15.6 KINETIC ENERGY

Kinetic energy for a system of particles is given by:

$$KE = \frac{1}{2} \sum_{j=1}^{n} m_j v_j^2, \qquad (15.16)$$

in an inertial frame of reference.

For a centroidal reference frame,

$$KE_{cm} = \frac{1}{2} mV_{cm}^2 + \frac{1}{2} \sum_{j=1}^{n} m_j v_j^2 \qquad (15.17)$$

Equation (15.17) shows that $KE_{cm}$ consists of two terms:

1) $\frac{1}{2}mV_{cm}^2$ = Kinetic Energy of the Mass Center,

2) $\frac{1}{2} \sum\limits_{j=1}^{n} m_j v_j^2$ = Kinetic Energy of the system's motion relative to the centroidal frame of reference.

# 15.7 CONSERVATION OF ENERGY

The principle of work and energy is written as follows which is simlar to that of the particle:

$$\boxed{W_{1 \to 2} = KE_2 - KE_1} \qquad (14.8)$$

$KE_2$ and $KE_1$ may be computed by either equation (15.16) or (15.17).

$W_{1 \to 2}$ is the work of the entire system. Internal and external forces must be considered.

If all the forces acting on the system are conservative, then equation (14.8) may be replaced by the following equation:

$$\boxed{KE_1 + PE_1 = KE_2 + PE_2 = E} \qquad (14.37)$$

This energy equation, as applied to the particle case, is also applicable to a system of particles.

# 15.8 IMPULSE AND MOMENTUM

Linear Impulse - Changes the linear momentum of the system.

Angular Impulse - Changes the angular momentum of the system:

$$\vec{P}_1 + \Sigma \int_{t_1}^{t_2} \vec{F}\,dt = \vec{P}_2; \qquad \vec{P}_1 = mV_{G_1}$$

$$(\vec{H}_0)_1 + \Sigma \int_{t_1}^{t_2} \vec{M}_0\,dt = (\vec{H}_0)_2; \qquad \vec{H}_0 = I_G w_1$$

(15.18)

When there are no external forces acting on a system:

$$\vec{P}_1 = \vec{P}_2$$

$$(\vec{H}_0)_1 = (\vec{H}_0)_2$$

(15.19)

Equations (15.19) represent conservation of momentum and are alternate forms of the equations (15.14) and (15.15).

# 15.9  CONTINUOUS SYSTEM

Consider the flow of fluid through a duct:

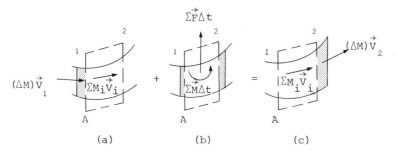

Fig. 15.2 Fluid Flow Through A Duct

153

Equation Formation:

The momentum of particles entering a constant area 'A' during a time '$\Delta t$' plus the impulses exerted during that time '$\Delta t$' is equipollent to the momentum of the particles leaving 'A' in time $\Delta t$:

$$(\Delta m)\vec{v}_1 + \Sigma\vec{F}\Delta t = (\Delta m)\vec{v}_2 \qquad (15.20)$$

Differential Equation of Motion:

$$\boxed{\Sigma\vec{F} = \dot{m}(\vec{v}_2 - \vec{v}_1)} \qquad (15.21)$$

Specific Cases:

### A) Fluid Diverted by a Vane

1) Fixed Vane - Direct application of the above relation.
   $\vec{F}$ = Force exerted by the vane on the fluid.

2) Vane Moving at Constant Velocity:

   a)  Choose a coordinate system moving with the vane.

   b)  $\vec{v}_1$ and $\vec{v}_2$ must be replaced by the relative velocities of the fluid with respect to the moving vane.

### B) Fluid Flowing Through a Pipe

In general, the pressure in the flow needs to be considered, therefore, the forces exerted on the area 'A' by the fluid on either side should be included in the analysis.

### C) Aircraft Turbine Engine

1) All velocities are relative to the engine.

2) The only external force considered is the force exerted by the engine on the air stream. This force is equal and opposite to the thrust.

### D) Aircraft Propeller

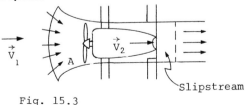

Fig. 15.3

154

1) Velocities are measured with respect to the aircraft.
$\vec{v}_1 \approx 0$

2) The flow rate is the product of $\vec{v}_2$ and the cross sectional area of the slipstream (see Figure 15.3).

3) The only external force considered is the thrust.

# 15.10 VARIABLE MASS SYSTEMS

From the principle of impulse and momentum:

$$\vec{F}\,\Delta t = (\vec{P})_{t+\Delta t} - (\vec{P})_t$$

(15.22)

General Differential Equation of Motion:

$$\vec{F} = m\,\frac{d\vec{v}}{dt} - \vec{u}\,\frac{dm}{dt}$$

(15.23)

where
$\vec{u}$ = Velocity of the Mass Gained (or Lost) Relative to the Moving Body

Specific Cases:

A) Mass Gaining Systems

In this case

$$\vec{u} = -\vec{v},$$

and equation (15.23) becomes:

$$\vec{F} = m\,\frac{d\vec{v}}{dt} + \vec{v}\,\frac{dm}{dt} = \frac{d(m\vec{v})}{dt}$$

(15.24)

Equation (15.24) is applicable only if the initial velocity of the mass gained is zero.

In equation (15.24) $v \frac{dm}{dt}$ represents the magnitude of force exerted by the mass gained. $\frac{dm}{dt}$ represents the rate at which the mass is gained.

B) Mass Loosing Systems - Rocket Motion

In this case:

$$\frac{dm}{dt} < 0,$$

Assume that $\vec{F} = 0$, then equation (15.23) becomes

$$m \frac{d\vec{v}}{dt} = \vec{u} \frac{dm}{dt} \qquad (15.25)$$

If u is constant, then equation (15.25) may be solved to obtain the value of v.

$$v = v_0 + u \ln \frac{M_0}{M} \qquad (15.26)$$

# CHAPTER 16


# KINEMATICS OF RIGID BODIES


## 16.1 INTRODUCTION

Types of Rigid Body Motion:

A) Translation - All particles of the body move in a straight (rectilinear) or curved (curvilinear) paths.

B) Rotation About a Fixed Axis - All the particles move in circular paths with their centers on a fixed straight line called the axis of rotation.

C) General Plane Motion - All particles in the body remain at constant distance from a fixed reference plane and move in parallel planes. All particles on the same straight line perpendicular to the reference plane have identical values of displacement, velocity and acceleration. Plane in which mass center moves is called plane of motion.

D) Motion About a Fixed Point - Here the distance from a fixed point to any particle of the body is constant. Therefore, the path of motion lies on a sphere and centered at the fixed point.

E) General Motion - All other motion.


## 16.2 TRANSLATION

For a body in translation:

A) The resultant of all applied forces passes through the mass center of the body.

B) All the particles of the body have the same velocity and acceleration at any given instant.

C) In rectilinear translation, velocity and acceleration have the same direction.

D) In curvilinear translation, velocity and acceleration change in direction and magnitude.

# 16.3 ROTATION

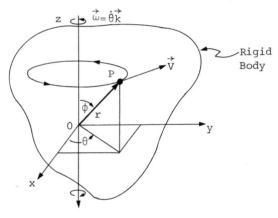

Fig. 16.1

The differential equations of rotation are analogous to the equations of translation:

| Translation | Rotation |
|---|---|
| $v = \dfrac{ds}{dt}$ | $\omega = \dfrac{d\theta}{dt}$ |
| $a = \dfrac{dv}{dt}$ | $\alpha = \dfrac{d\omega}{dt}$ |
| $ads = vdv$ | $\alpha d\theta = \omega d\omega$ |

158

Transformations:

$$s = r\,\theta$$
$$v = r\omega$$
$$a_t = r\,\alpha$$
$$a_n = r\,\omega^2$$

(16.1)

## Omega Theorem

The time derivative of a constant length vector fixed in a rotating body is equal to the cross product of the angular velocity with the vector. i.e.,

$$\frac{dr}{dt} = \vec{\omega} \times \vec{r}$$

where $\vec{\omega}$ = Angular Velocity, and

$\vec{r}$ = Constant Length Vector

For a point in the body (see Figure 16.1):

Velocity:

$$\boxed{\vec{v} = \frac{d\vec{r}}{dt} = \vec{\omega} \times \vec{r}}$$

(16.2)

Speed:

$$\boxed{v = \frac{ds}{dt} = r\,\dot{\theta}\sin\phi}$$

(16.3)

Acceleration:

$$\boxed{\vec{a} = \vec{\alpha} \times \vec{r} + \vec{\omega} \times (\vec{\omega} \times \vec{r})}$$

(16.4)

where

$$\vec{\alpha} = \frac{d\vec{\omega}}{dt} = \text{Angular Acceleration},$$

Also written as $\dot{\omega}\,\vec{k}$ or $\ddot{\theta}\,\vec{k}$

## Rotation of a Slab

The motion of a slab in a reference plane perpendicular to the axis of rotation is used to define the rotation of a rigid body about a fixed axis.

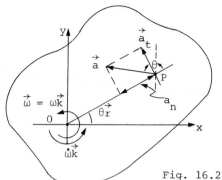

**For Point P:**

Fig. 16.2

Velocity:

$$\vec{v} = {}_\omega\vec{k} \times \vec{r}$$

(16.3)

Speed:

$$v = r\,{}_\omega$$

(16.1)

Acceleration:

$$\vec{a} = \dot{{}_\omega}\vec{k} \times \vec{r} - {}_\omega^2 \vec{r}$$

(16.4)

Tangential and Normal Acceleration:

$$\vec{a}_t = \dot{{}_\omega}\vec{k} \times \vec{r}$$
$$\vec{a}_n = -{}_\omega^2 \vec{r}$$

(16.5)

Equations of Motion:

$$\omega = \frac{d\theta}{dt}$$
$$\dot{\omega} = \frac{d^2\theta}{dt^2} = {}_\omega\frac{d\omega}{d\theta}$$

(16.6)

Special Cases:

A) Uniform Rotation where $\vec{\alpha} = 0$

    Angular coordinate is

160

$$\boxed{\theta = \theta_0 + \omega t} \qquad (16.7)$$

B) Uniformly Accelerated Rotation where $\bar{\alpha}$ = constant

$$\boxed{\begin{aligned} \omega &= \omega_0 + \alpha t \\ \theta &= \theta_0 + \omega_0 t + \tfrac{1}{2} \alpha t^2 \\ \omega^2 &= \omega_0^2 + 2\alpha(\theta - \theta_0) \end{aligned}} \qquad (16.8)$$

# 16.4 ABSOLUTE AND RELATIVE VELOCITY

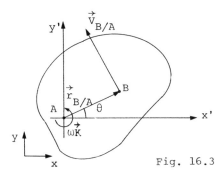

Fig. 16.3

Let $\vec{v}_{B/A}$ denote the velocity of B relative to A.

Relative Velcoity:

$$\boxed{\vec{v}_{B/A} = \omega \vec{k} \times \vec{r}_{B/A}} \qquad (16.9)$$

Relative Speed:

$$\boxed{v = r \dot{\theta} = r \omega} \qquad (16.10)$$

161

Absolute velocity of point B:

$$\boxed{\vec{v}_B = \vec{v}_A + \vec{v}_{B/A} = \vec{v}_A + (\omega\vec{k} \times \vec{r}_{B/A})} \qquad (16.11)$$

Absolute speed of point B:

$$\boxed{v_B = v_A + v_{B/A} = v_A + r\omega} \qquad (16.12)$$

# 16.5  INSTANTANEOUS CENTER OF ROTATION

Given a slab in general plane motion, the velocities of the particles composing the slab are the same as if the slab were rotating about a specific axis normal to the plane of the slab. This axis, known as the instantaneous axis of rotation is positioned at a point known as the instantaneous center of rotation.

Graphical Location of the Instantaneous Center of Rotation

**A) General Case**

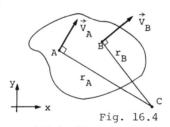

Fig. 16.4

**B) Parallel and Unequal Velocities**

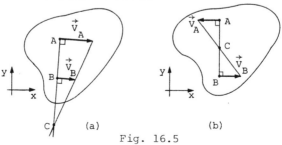

(a)                    (b)

Fig. 16.5

162

During the instantaneous rotation, all the particles have the same angular velocity about the instantaneous center. The velocities are directed normal to the line connecting the particles to the instantaneous center.

If the linear velocity and the angular velocity are known:

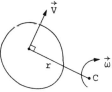

Fig. 16.6

Then C is located at:

$$r = \frac{V}{\omega}$$

(16.13)

For a Wheel or a Sphere:

C is located at distance equal to the radius R from the geometric center.

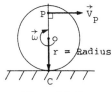

Fig. 16.7

Instantaneous Center of Zero Acceleration

A) It is used to compute acceleration in plane motion as if the body is in pure rotation about that point.

B) It is the same as the instantaneous center of rotation only for a body starting from rest.

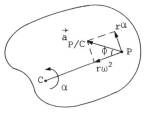

Fig. 16.8

163

$$a_p = a_c + a_{p/c}$$

When $\alpha$ and $\omega$ are known:

$$\boxed{\tan\phi = \frac{\alpha}{\omega^2}}$$  (16.14)

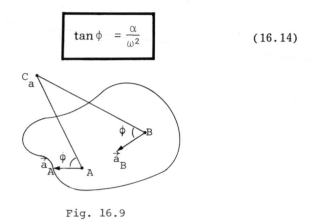

Fig. 16.9

$C_a$ = Instantaneous Center of Acceleration

# 16.6 ABSOLUTE AND RELATIVE ACCELERATION

Relative Acceleration Formula:

$$\boxed{\vec{a}_B = \vec{a}_A + \vec{a}_{B/A}}$$  (16.15)

Let $\vec{r}_{B/A}$ = Relative Position of B with Respect to A.

$\omega\vec{k}$ = Angular Velocity

$\alpha\vec{k}$ = Angular Acceleration

Tangential Compoment:

$$\boxed{(\vec{a}_{B/A})_t = \alpha\vec{k} \times \vec{r}_{B/A}}$$  (16.16)

Normal Compoment:

$$\boxed{(\vec{a}_{B/A})_n = -\omega^2 \vec{r}_{B/A}}$$  (16.17)

Scalar Equations of Equations (16.16) and (16.17):

$$\boxed{\begin{array}{l} (a_{B/A})_t = r\alpha \\ (a_{B/A})_n = r\omega^2 \end{array}}$$  (16.18)

Absolute Acceleration of B:

$$\boxed{\vec{a}_B = \vec{a}_A + [\alpha\vec{k} \times \vec{r}_{B/A} - \omega^2 \vec{r}_{B/A}]}$$  (16.19)

# 16.7 INERTIAL FORCES

If an accelerated coordinate system is used to describe the motion of a particle, then Newton's second law becomes:

$$\boxed{\vec{F} - m\vec{a}_0 = m\vec{a}}$$  (16.20)

where

$\vec{a}_0$ = Acceleration of the Coordinate System

The term $(-m\vec{a}_0)$ is the inertial or fictitious force term. It is not the result of any interaction with other bodies. It is the result of using an accelerated coordinate system.

# 16.8 NON-INERTIAL REFERENCE SYSTEM

Non-Inertial Coordinate System - When the reference frame

165

undergoes translation and rotation.

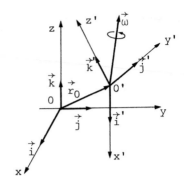

Fig. 16.10 Non Intertial
Reference System

In general, the absolute time derivative of any vector A in the rotating frame 0'x'y'z' is:

$$\left(\frac{d\vec{A}}{dt}\right)_{0xyz} = \left(\frac{d\vec{A}}{dt}\right)_{0'x'y'z'} + (\vec{\omega} \times \vec{A})$$  (16.21)

Equation (16.21) has two parts:

A) $\left(\frac{d\vec{A}}{dt}\right)_{0'x'y'z'}$ = Change of $\vec{A}$ with respect to the rotating system 0'x'y'z'.

B) $\vec{\omega} \times \vec{A}$ = Induced motion of the moving frame 0'x'y'z' with respect to the stationary system 0xyz.

By the principle stated in equation (16.21):

Velocity:

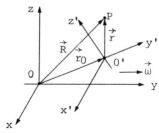

Fig. 16.11

$$\boxed{\vec{v}_p = \left(\frac{d\vec{R}}{dt}\right)_{0xyz} = (\dot{\vec{r}})_{0'x'y'z'} + \vec{\omega} \times \vec{r} + \vec{v}_0}$$

(16.22)

$\vec{v}_p$ = Absolute velocity of p

$(\dot{\vec{r}})_{0'x'y'z'}$ = Relative velocity of p with respect to the moving system

$\vec{\omega} \times \vec{r}$ = Induced motion due to rotation of $0'x'y'z'$

$\vec{v}_0 = \dfrac{d\vec{r}_0}{dt}$ = Absolute velocity of the moving origin $0'$ with respect to the fixed system $0xyz$

Acceleration - Found by differentiating equation (16.21)

with $\vec{A}$ equal to $\dfrac{d\vec{R}}{dt} - \vec{v}_0 = \dot{\vec{r}} + \vec{\omega} \times \vec{r}$:

$$\boxed{\begin{aligned}\vec{a}_p = \left(\frac{d^2 R}{dt^2}\right)_{0xyz} &= (\ddot{\vec{r}})_{0'x'y'z'} + [2\vec{\omega} \times (\dot{\vec{r}})_{0xyz}] \\ &+ (\dot{\vec{\omega}} \times \vec{r}) + [\vec{\omega} \times (\vec{\omega} \times \vec{r})] + \vec{A}_0\end{aligned}}$$

$\vec{a}_p$ = Absolute Acceleration of p,                     (16.23)

$(\ddot{\vec{r}})_{0'x'y'z'}$ = Relative acceleration of the particle with respect to the moving coordinate system

$2\vec{\omega} \times (\dot{\vec{r}})$ = Coriolis acceleration

$\dot{\vec{\omega}} \times \vec{r}$ = Transverse acceleration

$\vec{\omega} \times (\vec{\omega} \times \vec{r})$ = Centripetal acceleration

$\vec{A}_0 = \dfrac{d^2\vec{r}_0}{dt^2}$ = Absolute acceleration of the moving origin

Note: Coriolis, transverse, and centripetal acceleration are rotational terms which appear only in the fixed system $0xyz$.

Newton's Second Law

Equation (16.20) may now be written as

$$\vec{F} - m\vec{A}_0 - (2m\vec{\omega} \times \dot{\vec{r}}) - (m\dot{\vec{\omega}} \times \vec{r}) - m\vec{\omega} \times (\vec{\omega} \times \vec{r}) = m\ddot{\vec{r}}$$

(16.24)

In equation (16.24), the inertial terms are as follows:

Coriolis Force

$$\vec{F}_{cor} = -2m\vec{\omega} \times \dot{\vec{r}}$$

(16.25)

This force is always perpendicular to the velocity vector.

Transverse Force

$$\vec{F}_{trans} = -m\dot{\vec{\omega}} \times \vec{r}$$

(16.26)

This force is present only if there is an angular acceleration of the rotating reference system and acts normal to the position vector.

Centrifugal Force

$$\vec{F}_{cent} = -m\vec{\omega} \times (\vec{\omega} \times \vec{r})$$

(16.27)

This force acts normal to, and is directed away from the axis of rotation. Its magnitude is $mr\omega^2\sin\theta$.

Inertial forces from the rotation of the reference system are illustrated as follows:

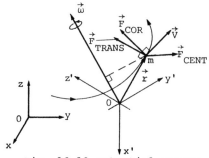

Fig. 16.12 Intertial Forces

# 16.9 MOTION ABOUT A FIXED POINT

In general, the displacement of a rigid body with respect to a fixed point 0 is equivalent to a rotation of the body about an axis through 0.

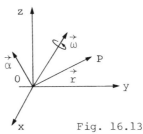

Fig. 16.13

Velocity:

$$\vec{v} = \frac{d\vec{r}}{dt} = \vec{\omega} \times \vec{r}$$

(16.28)

Acceleration:

$$\vec{a} = \vec{\alpha} \times \vec{r} + \vec{\omega} \times (\vec{\omega} \times \vec{r})$$

(16.29)

$\vec{\alpha} = \dfrac{d\vec{\omega}}{dt}$ – It represents the velocity of the tip of the vector $\vec{\omega}$.

# THE ENGLISH HANDBOOK
## OF
# GRAMMAR, STYLE,
## AND
# COMPOSITION

- This book illustrates the rules and numerous exceptions that are characteristic of the English language, in great depth, detail, and clarity.

- Over 2,000 examples comparing correct and wrong usage in all areas of grammar and writing.

- Solves the usual confusion about punctuation.

- Illustrates spelling "tricks" and how to remember correct spelling.

- Teaches how to acquire good writing skills.

- Provides special learning exercises at the end of each chapter to prepare for homework and exams.

- Fully indexed for locating specific topics rapidly.

Available at your local bookstore or order directly from us by sending in coupon below.

# HANDBOOK AND GUIDE
# FOR
# SELECTING A CAREER
## AND PREPARING FOR THE FUTURE

**NEW 1987-88 EDITION**

**For:**

- **Young Job-Seekers**
- **Persons Seeking a Career Change**
- **Persons Entering the Labor Force Later in Life**

**Over 250 careers are covered. Each career is described in detail including:**

- **Training and Education**
- **Character of the Work Performed**
- **Working Conditions**
- **Amount of Earnings**
- **Advancement Opportunities**
- **Prospects for the Future**

Available at your local bookstore or order directly from us by sending in coupon below.

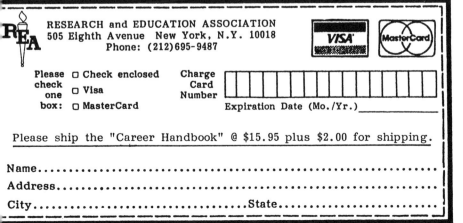

# THE PROBLEM SOLVERS

The "PROBLEM SOLVERS" are comprehensive supplemental textbooks designed to save time in finding solutions to problems. Each "PROBLEM SOLVER" is the first of its kind ever produced in its field. It is the product of a massive effort to illustrate almost any imaginable problem in exceptional depth, detail, and clarity. Each problem is worked out in detail with step-by-step solution, and the problems are arranged in order of complexity from elementary to advanced. Each book is fully indexed for locating problems rapidly.

ADVANCED CALCULUS
ALGEBRA & TRIGONOMETRY
AUTOMATIC CONTROL
  SYSTEMS/ROBOTICS
BIOLOGY
BUSINESS, ACCOUNTING,
  & FINANCE
CALCULUS
CHEMISTRY
COMPLEX VARIABLES
COMPUTER SCIENCE
DIFFERENTIAL EQUATIONS
ECONOMICS
ELECTRICAL MACHINES
ELECTRIC CIRCUITS
ELECTROMAGNETICS
ELECTRONIC COMMUNICATIONS
ELECTRONICS
FINITE and DISCRETE MATH
FLUID MECHANICS/DYNAMICS
GENETICS

GEOMETRY:
  PLANE • SOLID • ANALYTIC
HEAT TRANSFER
LINEAR ALGEBRA
MACHINE DESIGN
MECHANICS: STATICS • DYNAMICS
NUMERICAL ANALYSIS
OPERATIONS RESEARCH
OPTICS
ORGANIC CHEMISTRY
PHYSICAL CHEMISTRY
PHYSICS
PRE-CALCULUS
PSYCHOLOGY
STATISTICS
STRENGTH OF MATERIALS &
  MECHANICS OF SOLIDS
TECHNICAL DESIGN GRAPHICS
THERMODYNAMICS
TRANSPORT PHENOMENA:
  MOMENTUM • ENERGY • MASS
VECTOR ANALYSIS

If you would like more information about any of these books, complete the coupon below and return it to us or go to your local bookstore.

RESEARCH and EDUCATION ASSOCIATION
505 Eighth Avenue • New York, N.Y. 10018
         Phone: (212) 695-9487

         Please send me more information about your
         Problem Solver Books.

Name ........................................................................

Address .....................................................................

City ........................... State ...................................